WHO
WRECKED THE ROOF?

A Bible Mystery

The Scripture setting for this story
can be found in Matthew 9:1-8, Mark 2:1-12,
and Luke 5:17-26.

The Standard Publishing Company, Cincinnati, Ohio
A division of Standex International Corporation
Text © 1994 by Bob Hartman
Illustrations © 1994 by The Standard Publishing Company
All rights reserved. Printed in the United States of America
01 00 99 98 97 96 95 94   5 4 3 2 1
Library of Congress Catalog Card Number 94-9754
ISBN 0-7847-0189-X
Cataloging-in-Publication data available
Designed by Coleen Davis

WHO
WRECKED THE ROOF?

A Bible Mystery

by Bob Hartman
illustrated by Terri Steiger

STANDARD
PUBLISHING
Cincinnati, Ohio

Daniel dropped his stick sword and cringed when he heard
his father's angry call.
"He must know about the broken pots," Daniel said out loud.
There was nothing for a make-believe soldier to do but surrender.
So he lowered his head in defeat and marched into the house.

It was a beautiful house.
The best on the street.
Daniel's father had built it himself.
And many more houses
in Capernaum, as well.
Daniel's father was a good builder.
But Daniel seemed to be good
only at knocking things down.
"You broke three
of your mother's best pots today,"
said Daniel's father.
"What were you doing?"

"Saving our land from
the Roman invaders, Father."
Daniel's father cocked his head

and squinted at his son.
It was the same look he gave a wall,
to make sure he'd built it straight.

"What?"
"Me and Reuben were the freedom
fighters, and Adam and Josh were
the Romans. We had 'em on the run!
Then I swung my sword one last time,
and it sort of slipped out of my hand
and flew across the room — "
"And crashed into your mother's pots."
"Something like that," said Daniel.
Then he raised his head
and gave his father "the look."
The look that said,
"I'm sorry and I'll try not to do it again
but I probably will so won't you
forgive me anyway and try not to be
too angry, pleeeease!"

Daniel's father sighed.
He had seen "the look" the week before,
when Daniel scratched the front door.
And the week before that,
when Daniel knocked the dishes off the table.
And the week before that . . .

"That look won't work this time, son," he said, as sternly as he could.
"Every afternoon for the next week, you will come into my workshop.
You will put away the tools, and sweep the floor,
and you will not leave until the place is neat and clean.
It's about time you learned to fix things instead of tearing them up."
Then Daniel's father turned around and marched out of the house.

Daniel stood there for a moment,
staring at the floor.
He scratched his head.
"The look" was supposed to work.

Daniel's mother put her hand on his shoulder. "Your father has a lot on his mind," she said gently. "His work, taking care of this house, his sick friend . . . and, besides, we have told you not to play that fighting game indoors."

Next day, Daniel played hard
with his friends.
But he knew that all week,
the playing would have to
stop early.
That troubled him,
and when the time finally came
for him to go to the workshop,
it was almost a relief.

It was even more of a relief
when Daniel got to the workshop
and found no one there.
Well, a relief and a puzzle.
"Where is everybody?" he wondered.

And that's when Daniel heard
the shouting.
He ran outside and saw
an excited crowd
flooding into the street.

"What's happening?" yelled Daniel. "Where are you going?"
"To the house of Aaron the Pharisee," called back a young man.
"Jesus is there!" added a little girl.
"And he's making sick people well!" hollered an old blind woman,
holding tight to the arm of her friend.

Aaron the Pharisee's house? thought Daniel.
I know where that is. Father finished it just last month.
Daniel turned and called into the empty workshop,
"Does anyone here mind if I go and see
what's happening at Aaron's house?"
Then he jumped into the crowd that rushed
like a wave to the Pharisee's door.

Unfortunately, by the time Daniel got to Aaron's house,
it was already flooded with folk, and there was no room left inside.

He scooted
between legs.

Well, no room for most people.
Daniel just dropped to all fours
and crawled through the crowd
like they were the enemy line.

He wriggled
through gaps.

He used his make-believe
sword a time or two.

And finally he was there,
smack in the middle of Aaron's house —
not a stick sword's length from Jesus.

Daniel had never seen anything like it.
There was that old blind woman
he'd seen on the street.
She groped her way to Jesus,
her hands stretched out in front
so she wouldn't bump into anything.

The woman blinked once,
blinked twice,
and then she shouted,
"I can see! I can see!"
louder and louder,
over and over again.

Jesus took her hands and
placed them at her side.
Then he laid his own
hands on those old
blind eyes, he bowed
his head, and he
prayed. And when
he took away
his hands,
the woman's
eyes shone
bright
and blue.

She shouted so long,
Daniel put his hands over his ears.
She shouted so loud,
Daniel thought she would shout
the roof off the place.

And so she did.

Or so it seemed.
Bits and pieces of stuff
started to fall from the roof.
The old woman laughed
and pointed.
She was just happy
to be able to see it.

But all Daniel could think about was his father,
who had put that roof up there and would be
anything but pleased to see it coming down.
The pieces were getting bigger, and it was clear
that the woman's shouting had nothing to do with it.

Someone was wrecking the roof!

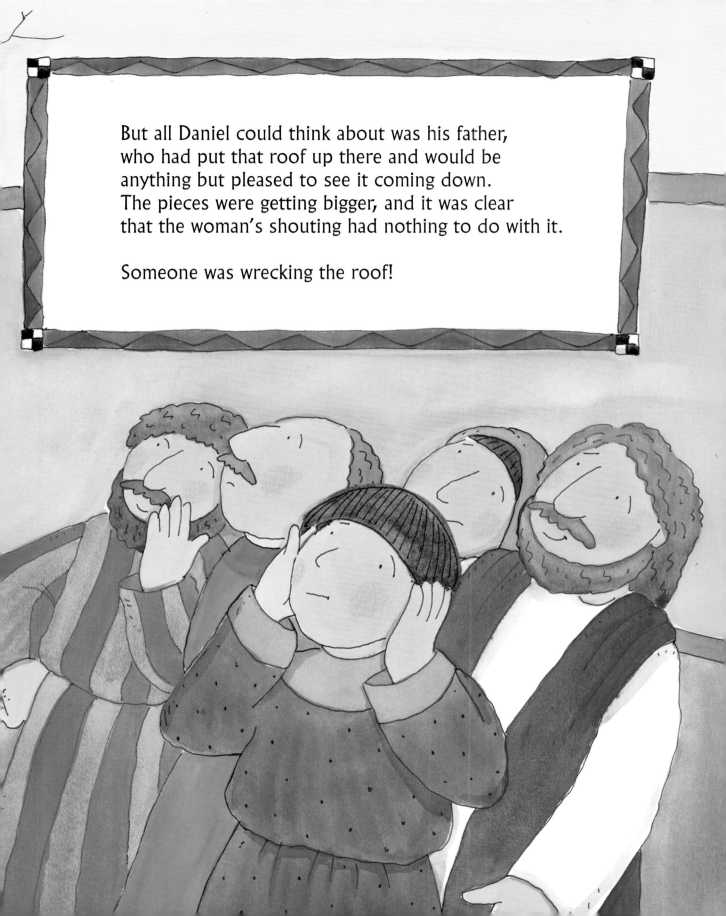

Jesus stepped back.
Aaron the Pharisee stepped forward.

And the once-blind woman
stepped out of the way.

Everyone else looked up at the roof. There were holes now, and hands — pairs of hands reaching through the holes to tear away those brand new titles and make one great hole out of many.

All Daniel could think about was what his father would say.

And how his father would look — red-faced, with his teeth clenched and his eyes dark, sharp slits.

And then Daniel saw his father.
But he wasn't in the crowd. He wasn't leaning through a window.
He was up there — peering down through the hole in the roof.
Daniel's father was wrecking his own roof!
And the look on his face. It wasn't the angry look Daniel had
imagined. Oh, no, it was "the look" — Daniel's look.
And it was aimed at one furious Pharisee.

"Now, Aaron," Daniel heard his father say, "I know I just put this roof on. But one of my men has been sick, and the sickness left him paralyzed. We tried to get in past the crowd, but we couldn't. And he needs to get in. He needs to see Jesus. This just seemed to be the most . . . practical way."
And then he added, in a perfect Daniel tone, "I'm sorry. I'll fix it. Free of charge."

Aaron grunted his approval, and Daniel's father and three of his friends lowered a man down to Jesus on a bed with strong ropes at each corner.

What did Jesus do?
He made the man well,
that's what.
So well he rolled up
his own bed.
So well he could have
climbed back out

"Daniel!" called a voice
from the roof.
"What are you doing here?"
Oops. Daniel had forgotten
about cleaning up the workshop.
Oh, well. He lowered his head
and marched out front to meet
his father.

that hole if he'd
wanted to.
But he walked through
the crowd, instead,
praising God,
with Daniel whooping
and hollering behind.

Daniel's father was wiping his hands and grinning.
"Good work is important," he said, "but good friends
are more important still."
"So I can go and play with my friends now,
instead of cleaning up your workshop?" asked Daniel,
trying out "the look" one last time.

"No," his father answered slowly. "I will have to take care of the mess I made today, and you still have to clean the workshop."

Then Daniel's father picked
him up and popped him on his
shoulders.
"But after we've finished,"
he said, "I don't see any reason
why you and I shouldn't both spend
some time with our friends."

Daniel pulled out his stick sword
and swung it 'round his head.
"Charge!" he shouted,
and Daniel and his father galloped
together all the way home.